Mind Over Matter

Ellen Tutton

BookLeaf
Publishing

India | USA | UK

Presentation by *BookLeaf Publishing*

Web: www.bookleafpub.com

E-mail: info@bookleafpub.com

ISBN: 9789360942083

First edition 2024

To the 6,048 individuals who have received an MS diagnosis in the 21 days it took to write 21 poems:

Remember, there are others who understand and stand with you. You're not facing this alone. Not now, not tomorrow, not ever.

ACKNOWLEDGEMENT

This book you see before you is a direct result of a night drinking with my best friends, a night my soul needed but also a night that took me on this unexpected adventure of writing poems for the first time in many, many years.

So, to my friends - thank you for being a contributing factor to the mood I was in when I embarked on a poem writing challenge after too many proseccos.

PREFACE

When facing my MS diagnosis, the toughest part was explaining the unexplainable to others. Throughout my years as a dedicated patient advocate and health consultant, I've witnessed the difficulty many face in putting invisible MS symptoms and the emotions surrounding the diagnosis into words.

In my pursuit to redefine how we convey the unique experience of living with MS, I have created this collection of poems.

'Mind Over White Matter' is a journey we will share together, embracing some of the realities that I and 2.8 million individuals worldwide experience as we navigating life with this condition.

Lighthouse of the Brain

My brain, a lighthouse,
That guides my vessel to shore,
But the lighthouse light now flickers,
Sometimes it is off, no more.

When it is on, I still feel unsafe.
Will it falter again?
Sending signals not intended,
To navigate harsh terrain.

When the journey seems a risk,
No option but to pause.
The chaos and destruction,
Continuing could cause.

Relying on other people's beacons,
When my light is redundant,
Is both a blessing and a curse,
A burden in abundance.

For if the lighthouse's light,
Cannot guide my vessel to shore,
I will find a way to get there,
Adapting, a detour.

Neurologist Appointment

There's inflammation,
Abbreviation MS,
See you next clinic.

Falling for You

Falling for you.
I stumble over my words,
I get giddy when you're here.
The room starts spinning,
My ears are ringing,
Songs I cannot un-hear.

I forget what my life was before.
I think of our future often.
You keep me awake at night,
I feel your weight upon me,
Blinded by your touch,
Your hug so very tight.

There are rumors that you'll leave!
I don't believe them true.
Lost in you, I forget my own name.
My nerves make me shake.
Spontaneous and unpredictable,
No two days the same.

I get weak at the knees,
A lump in my throat,
A shiver down my spine.
My life feels off balance.

You're tattooed on my brain,
Every day since you were mine.

Luck

How lucky I am.
I understand the value of health,
Not something to take for granted.
How lucky I am.
To have met so many new friends,
That have blossomed since being planted.

How lucky I am.
To have traveled the world,
Amplifying the voices unheard.
How lucky I am.
Having access to treatment,
Not just an option, but my preferred.

How lucky I am.
With the support that I have,
We have taken this on together.
How lucky I am…
To have this illness.
One that will last forever.

How lucky am I?
Or is luck just a word,
To make us feel grateful inside?
Is this really luck?

Or just one of those things,
That I should take in my stride?

Because lucky I am.
But also, I'm not.
Everything that I want,
Is not everything that I've got.

Sweet Dreams

Insomnia, my friend in darkness and enemy in light.
You keep my mind racing, deep in thought when the world is silent.
You slow me down when the world is awake.
You are an end with no beginning to the rest that I need.

I will not listen to your words that echo through my head.
The power that you have to control my mind's desire.
The power that you have to drain all of mine.
The power that you have.

I'll see you again.

Tomorrow.

Insomnia.

My friend.

No Feeling

To not feel sorrow,
Instead, relief.
Thanks to Google,
MS was already my belief!

I'd mentally prepared,
Despite speculation.
I felt ready for answers,
No shock or devastation.

My body felt alien,
I didn't feel in control.
It was happening to me,
But I had others to console.

Days of confusion.
Dazed and fatigued.
Not getting better,
My future hard to conceive.

Moments of normality,
Gradually arrived by the day.
But never fully returned,
Some symptoms would stay.

And now, my emotions,
8 years along,
Feature grief and excitement,
Neither of which is wrong.

I miss the old me.
The freedom and ignorance.
But new me is powerful.
My story is not a coincidence!

Control

Clamp shackles to my ankles,
With weights I cannot move.
I'll drag my legs rather than rest,
As if I have something to prove.

Restrict the blood flow to my arm,
Until pins and needles occur.
I won't be knitting, can't hold a thing,
Use of both hands I'd prefer.

Block my mouth with tape,
So words cannot form scripts.
My thoughts won't be aloud,
No secrets will pass my lips.

Drain my battery completely,
Then make me climb a hill.
Keep shoveling tasks at me,
Being this fatigued is a skill.

Set alarms off in my ears,
Let the ringing drill inside.
I want peace in my head,
That only loud places will provide.

Shake me so violently,
That my body feels detached.
I cannot control the motion,
There's no feeling to be matched.

Drown my bladder with water,
Fill it with urgency.
Open the floodgate without warning,
Make me react to this emergency.

Wake me up each morning,
Not knowing what to expect.
How will you play with me today?
What will be your effect?

The Thing

Pass me the thing.
The thing.
Not that thing!
The thing.
That thingy,
Over there.
You know what I mean.
There!
That!
Thing.
…What do you call it?

Next to the box.
No, not that box.
That box.
Yes, I know it's a tray,
That's what I said.
Next to that.

Pass me the thing.
The thing.
Not that thing.
The thing.
The button thing.
You know?

That gets the menu up,
On the TV.
The programme changer thing,
That thing.

'What, this?
The remote?'

Eclipse of the Mind

Forever present,
Even when shadows casted.
Whole but crescent moon.

Internal Earthquakes

7.8 on the Richter scale,
An earthquake through the core.
A simple movement triggered,
Warnings given to no avail.

Vision focused on the floor,
Surrounding, they stayed still.
The tremors weren't external,
This, an internal battle, a war.

An arm, a leg, violently lashes,
Cramping will settle in its place.
Longing for stillness, in fear,
Unprepared for when the aftershock crashes.

The magnitude is far greater than billed,
A tsunami in its wake.
Destruction everywhere it touched,
Time needed to rebuild.

Age of Time

We'll meet.
We'll say, 'let's do this more often'.
Life gets in the way,
We won't stick to our word.

It feels easier now,
Not sticking to our words.
Your commitments are bigger than before,
A husband, child, a job, and more.

But years ago, this wasn't the case.
No equal playing field,
For me to embrace.

Instead, it was,
'I'm sorry'
'I can't'
'I'm busy'

Another excuse.
More lies being told.

Because how could I say,
'It's hard even to get through a day.'

Saying no,
To an evening,
A night,
A weekend between,
The truth remains the same.

Although seeing you would fill my cup,
My cup would also drain.

Get a Grip

Hard to get a grip.
Mentally and physically.
Clinging to unknown.

Two

Not disabled enough for benefits.
Too disabled for a promotion.
Hide my identity,
Or cause a commotion?

I don't look disabled,
The Equality Act says that I am.
No traditional mobility aids,
Mine's pushing a trolley or pram.

Able to get dressed,
Look good in what I wear.
But nothing with buttons,
And always unkempt hair.

There are two sides to my story,
Neither one lesser or more.
A continuum of misperception.
A beauty and a flaw.

Hope

Worrying is suffering twice.
You can't escape the worry,
But it helps if you try.
Because 'why' doesn't solve it,
'What if' doesn't change a thing.
Just focus on moving forward.
Focus on the good the future can bring!

Invisible

Sit on your hand.
Wear shoes a size too small.
Spin around really fast.
Look over the edge of a skyscraper building.
Walk on wet tarmac.
Stay awake for 72 hours.
Fall asleep during the day.
Stand on a vibrating plate.
Play music too loud, then sit in silence.
Wear an itchy jumper.
Do a weekly shop without a shopping list.
Drink so much you slur your words.
Run so far that your legs feel detached.

While you do all the above, function as normal.
Go to work.
Socialise.
Raise a family.
Find time to cook, clean, eat.
Don't forget self-care.

Make it work.
Don't show cracks.
Deal with it silently,
The invisible illness within.

Tired

I'm tired.
Tired of explaining what my tired is.
Tired of hearing 'don't go to bed so late',
Or 'you don't know what tired is,' said with
hate.

I'm tired.
Tired of assumptions of why I am.
Tired of seeing eye rolls across the table.
Whispers saying 'she's lazy,' not knowing I'm
disabled.

I'm tired.
Tired of trying to stay awake.
When others were up all night with a screaming
child,
According to them, my tired is 'mild.'

I'm tired.
Tired of the response being 'you say that a lot.'
It's true I do, because fatigue is not as
commonly known.
So calling it tired makes me feel less alone.

Battlefield

What does it mean, what does any of this mean?
I've been dropped off in a war zone,
Told to pick a weapon, with no training, no time
to digest the situation at hand.
What if I pick the wrong one?
People around me share their opinions,
Some concerned,
Some excited,
Some indifferent.

I reach for the weapon that looks like it will
keep me safest for the longest,
In the distance, I can see more weapons, better
weapons.
As soon as I could lift a foot off the ground,
A blow to the head stops me in my tracks.
The commander's hand slides off my face and
onto my shoulder,
Holding me back.

'You've made your choice, now see it through.'
Months would follow of hiding in the shadows,
Avoiding conflict, praying that the weapon
picked will buy me time.

When an opportunity opens, I appear from the darkness,
On a quest to find something better.

The commander sees me and blocks my way,
Telling me all the reasons that I should stay.
But I can't.
I put up a fight,
I flee the scene,
Out of sight.
As I arrive closer to the weapons I envy,
A gatekeeper stands awaiting my presence,
They size me up, weapon and all.

I take a deep breath as anxiety consumes me.
The keeper lets me in upon my plea,
They point to all the options available for taking,
I sit and ponder for a moment, thinking of the possibilities.
Not only an upgrade to keep me safe,
But also,
An offering of hope,
In this battlefield I'm in.

Not a Life Sentence

At first I didn't see anyone like me.
The world suggested I was too young,
A diagnosis not for those whose life's just
begun.

As time went on, I started to see,
More representation,
More people looking like me.

Those with the same interests,
Drinking with friends until 3am,
Not running marathons, I could never be them!

Not because of my MS,
Just running isn't my style.
Enjoying unhealthy in my 20s for a while.

I can look after myself better,
When future years come along,
Even in my 30s I'll see nothing wrong.

Indulging sometimes, breaking the rules.
Accepting the fallout of your actions,
Because having fun is worth the reaction.

I just have to plan in different ways.
Assess the risk in all my decisions,
Not restricting my life like I was in prison.

Although this is with me for life,
It's not a life sentence.
So, I give myself grace and don't treat this with
vengeance.

Home

My heart feels like it's home,
As you giggle when I'm tying your shoelaces.

I only hope that you will never have to help me
tie mine.

Response

How do I tell you?
How do I break the news?
If the shoe were on the other foot,
I think I'd know what I would say.

'Take this day by day,
I'll be with you every step.
I don't know a lot, and I don't understand,
But what I do know is that you are a force,
And I'll be your helping hand.
This might change parts of you,
But I'll love those parts the same.
I'll be there through the good days,
And bad days; there will be zero shame.
It's not your fault,
You know that, right?
We will take this on together,
I'll advocate for you if you can't fight.
Every page of every book,
I'll continuously try and learn.
Anything you need, it's really no bother.
I can't imagine your concern.'

At least that's what I hope I'd say.
I don't think the same is true for you.

You'll probably tell me about your mums, best
friends, aunt,
The one whose hairdresser has MS.
You'll tell me they are cured after doing yoga six
times a day,
Eating clean,
And praying it away.
You'll tell me they climbed a mountain,
And I could too.
A positive mental attitude will see me through.
You'll recommend some insoles you saw online,
You'll start a GoFundMe in my honor,
Tell me I'm inspirational,
And ask me how long until I'm a goner.

I know you mean well, but you'll be a cliché.
I'll bite my tongue and pray; you'll just respond
with something not so bad, like
'I don't know what to say,'
Or
'I hope you're okay.'

Multiple

I have multiple things:
A job,
A house,
Friends,
A husband,
And a son.

I have multiple things,
And of all of my things,
Multiple Sclerosis is merely one.